Caribbean Supper Club
Recipe Book

 By Monica Cudjoe & Lee Sylvester

This edition published in 2012 by Tan Rosie Foods Ltd
Tan Rosie Foods Ltd
PO Box 15865
Birmingham
B23 3JB
UK

Follow Tan Rosie on twitter: twitter.com/tanrosie
Add Tan Rosie on Facebook: facebook.com/tanrosie

Text: Monica Cudjoe & Lee Sylvester
Photographer: Lee Sylvester
Designer: Lee Sylvester

ISBN 978-0-9572771-0-6

You can buy this book directly from the publisher at www.tanrosie.com
This book is also available to download in ebook format from Amazon.com

Contents

This recipe book is dedicated to the memory of Priscilla Rosanna "Tan Rosie" Cudjoe, from Carriacou, Grenada.
Beloved mother, tanty, grandmother and great grandmother.

Introduction

Whilst growing up in Carriacou, Grenada, I have always had a fascination with cooking especially with the abundance of fresh fruit, vegetables and fish that surrounded me in the Caribbean.

Food is something which has always brought my family together through big celebrations to small family gatherings.

Since my children were young, we have always had a big family and friends barbeque at my home. These are fantastic occasions where everyone can meet, chat, reminisce and most importantly eat great Caribbean food!

Since starting up our business in 2010, my daughter Lee and I discovered the idea of 'Supper Clubs' and decided to give it a whirl. Supper clubs started off in Cuba they're called "Paladres" whereby local house wives open up their homes for paying guests to eat their traditional home cooked meals.

Supper Clubs are popping up all around the UK and it's a great way to eat great food by 'home cooks.' It's also a brilliant way to meet and chat to like-minded 'foodies' in a friendly relaxed environment.

Our first supper club evening in 2011 was based around the culinary delights of my home country Grenada. We thought it would be a great idea to offer our guests a chance to sample some of the dishes that I grew up with as a child. The response was phenomenal! We have had an amazing set of guests dining in our living room and we've made some great friends in the process.

All of our supper club recipes are authentic Caribbean dishes, many of which have my own unique twist. They are very easy to follow and very tasty.

Caribbean cuisine is a fusion of many cultures such as African, English, French, Dutch, Indian, Spanish and Chinese. Contrary to popular belief, Caribbean food is not all 'hot.' We use chillies, namely 'scotch bonnet peppers' where necessary and in different amounts. We use a mixture of hot (scotch bonnet pepper) and sweet spices such as cinnamon, nutmeg (native to Grenada) and allspice (pimento).

There are common dishes that are eaten in most Caribbean islands such as, rice and peas, coo coo (polenta) and curry goat, but each island has it's own unique regional difference which makes Caribbean cuisine extremely varied and exciting.

Monica Cudjoe, Tan Rosie Foods

Sorrel Drink
with Cassava, Plantain & Sweet Potato Crisps with Sweet Chilli Sauce

Appetizers

Corn Fritters

These delicious Corn Fritters are a typical dish that has been cooked within my family kitchen back in Carriacou, Grenada since I can remember. It's a great way to use up fresh corn on the cob and it makes a great tasting snack.

Makes 24

Ingredients:
4 Fresh Sweet Corn Cobs
4 Spring Onions chopped
2 Red Chillies chopped
1 tsp Salt
1 tsp Black Pepper
1 Beaten Egg
1 Cup Plain flour or Channa Flour
1tsp Baking Powder
Cooking Oil for deep frying
1tbsp Fresh Coriander chopped
Water to combine

Method:
1. Remove Corn from cob using a sharp knife and place in a mixing bowl.
2. Add all other ingredients (except water) to corn.
3. Mix all ingredients together
4. Blend in water and mix to a "dropping" consistency.
5. Let mixture rest for 10 minutes
6. Heat oil in deep fryer and drop spoonfuls of the mixture into the hot oil and fry until golden brown.
7. Remove from the fryer with a slotted spoon and place on absorbent paper towels.
8. Serve with a Chilli Lime Sauce (page 20).

Sweet Potato Fritters

Sweet Potato fritters are a great staple food in the Caribbean. These taste fantastic with dipping sauces either sweet or hot with a fresh salad.

Makes 24

Ingredients:
8oz White Sweet Potato grated
4 Spring Onions chopped finely
1 Red Chilli chopped finely
1tsp Salt
1tsp Black Pepper
1tsp Baking Powder
1Cup Gram Flour
½ tsp Cumin Seeds toasted
½ tsp Fennel Seeds toasted
Water to mix
Vegetable Oil for deep frying
1tbsp Fresh Coriander chopped

Method:
1. Blend all ingredients together in a large mixing bowl.
2. Add water to blend to a "dropping" consistency.
3. Deep fry in vegetable oil by dropping spoonfuls of the mixture and fry until golden brown.
4. Drain on a kitchen paper and serve with a dipping sauce.

Plantain Crisps

Plantain crisps are a Caribbean classic. They are a great snack and can be made in advance and stored for eating at a later date. They taste great with a dipping sauce or with a dusting of sea salt.

Serves 12

Ingredients:

2-3 Green Plantains sliced thinly (a food processor using the slicing attachment is ideal or a mandolin).
Lime Juice or Lemon Juice
Salt
Oil for deep frying

Method:

1. Place sliced green plantain in a bowl and add a couple of pinches of salt, lemon or lime juice and a little water - mix and leave for 10-15 minutes.
2. Remove from bowl and dry well before deep frying.
3. Fry until crisp.
4. Turn out onto absorbent kitchen paper.
5. Serve with Pineapple & Mint Sauce (page 21).

Tips:

1. When crisps are cooked, they can be placed in an airtight container until ready. The container must be airtight or the crisps will be soft.
2. The crisps can be twice cooked to achieve a crispier texture.
3. You can also use Sweet Potatoes, Cassava or Yucca using the same method.

Phoulourie

Phoulourie are a traditional Trinidadian snack food. They are particularly delicious served with a chutney of your choice such as Mango or a Tamarind Chutney or sauce. They can be eaten as a snack or as a starter dish.

Makes 24

Ingredients:

1 Cup Gram Flour
1 Garlic Clove minced
½ tsp Ground Tumeric
¼ tsp Ground Cumin
4 tsp Baking Powder
2 Cups Plain Flour
1tsp Salt
½ tsp Cayenne Pepper
2 Cups Oil for deep frying
Water
1tbsp Fresh Coriander

Method:

1. Combine all ingredients into a large mixing bowl.
2. Mix together with water to a "dropping" consistency.
3. Leave to rest for 15 minutes.
4. Heat oil in deep frying pan or wok.
5. Drop spoonfuls of the mixture into the hot oil.
6. Fry Phoulourie until golden brown, turning frequently.
7. Remove from the oil and drain on absorbent kitchen paper.

Accras (Salt Fish Fritters)

Accras or Salt Fish Fritters are a very common snack food in the Caribbean. If we are having a family party, we always have salt fish fritters on the menu. We eat these with a mild or hot chilli dip and they taste great with a salad as a starter. Try and eat them hot or warm, as the flavours taste better.

Makes 24

Ingredients:
8oz Salt Cod
1 Cup Plain Flour
1tsp Baking Powder
2 Eggs beaten
½ tsp Salt
½ tsp Black Pepper
1 tbsp Fish Sauce
1 Red Chilli minced
1 Green Chilli minced
4 Spring Onions finely chipped
1tbsp Fresh Thyme leaves
Milk to combine
Vegetable Oil for shallow frying
1 Lemon

Method:
1. Soak salt cod overnight in cold water and juice of lemon and change water twice.
2. Next day, drain salt cod, pour over boiling water and let steep for 10-15 minutes - then drain.
3. Flake salt cod.
4. Combine all other ingredients in a bowl and mix well (the mixture can be blended in a food processor for a finer texture). The batter should be "dropping" consistency.
5. Heat oil in shallow frying pan to medium heat.
6. Drop spoonfuls of the mixture into the frying pan and cook until golden brown, turning occasionally.
7. Remove from heat with slotted spoon and place on a dish lined with absorbent kitchen paper.
8. Serve while still hot or warm.

Sauces

Sweet Chilli Sauce

This has been a firm favourite from our Supper Club events. It's a great dipping sauce that's perfect with fritters and crisps. It's also very quick and easy to make.

Ingredients:
1 Cup Sugar
½ Cup Rice Wine Vinegar
½ Cup Water
2 Red Chillies finely chopped
Chopped Fresh coriander

Method:
1. Place sugar, water and rice wine vinegar in a pan and slowly bring to the boil.
2. Reduce heat and simmer for 5 minutes until reduced down.
3. Add chopped chillies and cook for a further 5 minutes.
4. Remove from heat and add coriander.
5. Allow to cool and serve.

Spicy Banana Chutney

We love this banana chutney recipe. It's spicy and tasty and it's superb with curries or strong cheeses and a glass of red wine!

Ingredients:
1kg Ripe Bananas peeled and chopped
1 Scotch Bonnet Pepper, de seeded and finely chopped
2 Garlic Cloves
250g finely chopped Onions
500g Soft Brown Sugar
225g Finely grated Ginger
2tsp Allspice
1tsp Cinnamon
400mls Malt Vinegar
1tsp Salt

Method:
1. In a preserving pan, place vinegar, onions, garlic, ginger and pepper. Slowly bring to the boil, stirring occasionally.
2. When brought to boil, reduce heat and simmer gently until onions are soft.
3. Add sugar, bananas allspice, cinnamon and salt.
4. Simmer until sugar has dissolved.
5. Turn up heat to medium and stir frequently until mixture thickens.
6. Pour into sterilized jars and seal.

Spiced Tomato Sauce

We've always made our own tomato sauce and it tastes so much better than a shop bought variety. Of course, if you'd like some heat add some finely chopped Scotch Bonnet Pepper to the mixture. We used this sauce with our Macaroni Pie (page 64) to add extra flavour to the dish.

Ingredients:
2 Cups Chopped Fresh Tomatoes, skinned (2 tins chopped tomatoes may be used)
1 Cup Finely chopped Onions
3 Cloves Garlic, minced
¼ Cup Olive Oil
50g Butter
1 tsp Sugar
¼ tsp Salt
1 Vegetable stock cube
1 tsp Dried Oregano
1 tsp Dried Thyme
1 tbsp Chopped Fresh Basil
1 tbsp Tomato puree
½ Cup Water

Method:
1. On medium heat, place saucepan with olive oil and butter to melt.
2. Add onions and sauté for 5 minutes, stirring occasionally.
3. Add garlic and chilli, then stir for 1 minute.
4. Add tomatoes, sugar, vegetable stock, dried herbs, water, salt and pepper.
5. Bring to the boil and simmer gently, stirring occasionally for 30 minutes.
6. Add tomato puree and basil.
7. Continue to simmer for a further 5-10 minutes.
8. Adjust seasoning to taste.

Tip:
The sauce should be of a thick consistency.
To obtain a smooth sauce, blend with a stick blender until smooth.

Onion Gravy

This onion gravy is a great accompaniment to our vegetarian Caribbean Style Nut Roast (page 59) we served up for a Christmas Supper Club event. It's got great flavour and a nice level of heat too, but not too hot! You can also use this recipe to add to your traditional Sunday roast dinner.

Ingredients:
1 Cup Onions finely chopped
1 Clove Garlic minced
1 tsp Fresh Thyme
2 Cups Water
1 tbsp Vegetable Stock
1 tbsp Plain Flour
1 tbsp Olive Oil
50g Butter
½ tsp Salt
½ tsp Black pepper
1 tsp Sugar
1 Chilli finely chopped

Method:
1. Place pan over medium heat, add olive oil and butter then stir until melted.
2. Add minced onion, sauté until golden brown.
3. Add thyme and chilli, then stir for 1 minute.
4. Add flour and cook through for 2 minutes.
5. Add water stirring as mixture thickens. Add more water if needed.
6. Continue stirring and add vegetable stock.
7. Cook through for about 10 minutes.
8. Season to taste.

Chilli Lime Sauce

Another favourite of our Supper Club! Limes are used extensively in Carriacou, Grenada. They taste fantastic in this sauce recipe especially with a kick of chilli. You can use the sauce with fritters, crisps and burgers. Also, the sauce tastes great with BBQ chicken wings!

Ingredients:
1 Cup Sugar
3 Quarter Cup Water
Juice and grated zest of 3 Limes
1 Red Chilli finely chopped
1 tbsp Chopped fresh coriander
¼ Cup Rice Wine Vinegar

Method:
1. Place sugar, water, juice of lemon and rice wine vinegar into a saucepan and bring to boil.
2. Reduce heat and simmer for 5 Minutes
3. Add chopped chilli, zest of lemon and continue to simmer for 5 minutes.
4. Remove from heat and add chopped coriander and serve when cool.

Pineapple & Mint Sauce

The acidity of pineapple with mint make for a great sauce. You can use it with any kind of fried dishes from burgers, sausages to samosas.

Ingredients:
2 Cups Fresh Pineapple finely chopped
1 Cup Sugar
½ Cup Water
¼ Cup Rice Wine Vinegar
1 Cup Chopped fresh mint leaves
1 Red Chilli finely chopped
¼ tsp Salt
¼ tsp Black Pepper
2 tbsp Chopped fresh Coriander

Method:
1. In a saucepan place pineapple, sugar, chillies, salt, black pepper, water and rice wine vinegar and simmer for 5 minutes.
2. Remove pan from heat then add half the chopped mint and coriander then allow to cool.
3. Add remainder of mint when cool.

Mango Mojo Sauce

Mango Mojo is a traditional Cuban sauce. It can be used with a variety dishes to enhance any meal. We've used this sauce to accompany our Supper Club appetizers such as fritters and crisps, which always goes down well with our guests.

Ingredients:

2 Large mangoes peeled and chopped
8 Cloves of garlic finely minced
¼ Cup extra virgin olive oil
¼ Cup freshly squeezed lime juice
¼ Cup freshly squeezed orange juice
¼ tsp ground cumin
¼ tsp Cayenne Pepper
Salt & Black pepper to season

Method:

1. On a medium heat, place oil in saucepan add minced garlic and stir for about 30 seconds without boiling - it is just to fragrant the oil.
2. Add lime juice, orange and combine by stirring.
3. Add cumin, salt, pepper, cayenne pepper and diced mango.
4. Bring to the boil and simmer gently for about 5 minutes stirring occasionally to prevent sticking.
5. Check for seasoning and cool for 5 minutes.
6. In a glass bowl pour sauce and let it rest covered.
7. Allow sauce to rest for 2-4 hours before serving. This allows flavours to blend well. The sauce should thicken on cooling.

Tip:

This sauce can be kept in the fridge for up to 1 week.

Mixed Pepper Creole Sauce

We use this Creole sauce with Coo Coo (polenta) and Salt Fish (page 26). It's very traditional in the Caribbean to use this sauce with any kind of fish especially if it's fried. It's very easy and quick to make and tastes amazing.

Ingredients:
1 Red pepper cut in strips
1 Green Pepper cut into strips
1 Yellow Pepper cut into strips
1 Small red chilli chipped finely
2 Cloves garlic minced finely
1 tsp Fresh thyme leaves
¼ Cup Olive Oil
Salt & Black Pepper to taste
¼ tsp Sugar
1oz Butter
1 Cup diced tomato, deseeded and peeled

Method:
1. Place saucepan on medium heat.
2. Add oil and butter.
3. Add onion and sauté for 5 minutes until soft, stirring occasionally.
4. Add garlic and fry for 1 minute, stirring to prevent sticking.
5. Add peppers and cook for 5 minutes.
6. Add tomatoes, thyme, chilli, salt, pepper and sugar, stirring.
7. Cook for 5 minutes or until sauce reduces to a slightly thickish consistency.
8. Remove from heat and serve.

Supper Club guests - Jamaican Kitchen 2011

Starters

Salt Fish with Coo Coo & Creole Sauce

Salt fish and Creole sauce is a very traditional Caribbean dish which can be eaten as a main dish, starter or for breakfast. The sweet peppers really give the dish extra flavour and adds a beautiful colour to the dish.

Serves 6

Ingredients:
8oz Salted Cod
1 Large Onion finely chopped
1 Garlic Clove finely minced
1 tbsp Fresh thyme chopped
50g Butter
30mls Olive Oil
3 Tomatoes peeled de seeded and chopped
1 Red pepper sliced
1 Yellow pepper sliced
1 Green pepper sliced
Salt & Black pepper
1 Scotch Bonnet Pepper

Method:
1. Soak salt cod in cold water overnight, changing the water twice to remove excess salt.
2. Soak salt cod in boiling water for 1 hour.
3. Remove from water.
4. Remove skin, bones and flake cod fish.
5. In saucepan place oil and butter.
6. Place chopped onions in a pan and sauté for 5-10 minutes without colouring.
7. Add minced garlic and continue to sauté for 1 minute without browning, add peppers and cook for 5 minutes.
8. Add salt fish and whole scotch bonnet pepper and continue to cook through for approximately 3-5 minutes.
9. Season to taste with salt and pepper and remove scotch bonnet pepper.

Coo Coo Method:
See page 48.

Pure de Calabaza
(Creamy Pumpkin Soup)

This is a great Cuban style pumpkin soup recipe which we had on our menu for our Cuban Supper Club night. It went down a storm with our guests! The colour looks amazing and it tastes great too. Serve with some warm bread rolls.

Serves 6

Ingredients:
2 tbsp Olive oil
1 Large onion finely chopped
3 Garlic Cloves minced
1kg Pumpkin peeled, de seeded and cut into cubes
1 Small scotch bonnet pepper de seeded and finely chopped
4 Cups vegetable stock
1 Cup single cream
Salt & Black pepper to taste
Chopped chives for decoration (optional)

Method:
1. In a large saucepan, place olive oil and bring to the heat.
2. Add onions and sauté for 5 minutes without colouring.
3. Add garlic and scotch bonnet pepper and continue to sauté for 1 minute.
4. Add pumpkin and vegetable stock, bring to the boil then reduce heat and simmer for 30 minutes until pumpkin is tender.
5. Using a stick blender, place mixture into a jug and blend until smooth.
6. Return soup mixture to saucepan, add cream, salt and black pepper to taste.
7. Reheat and serve in warmed bowls, with a swirl of cream and chopped chives as decoration.

Balchi di Pisca
(Salt Cod Balls)

Salt cod balls are a very popular dish in Aruba. We had this dish as a starter for our Aruban supper club night and we served it with a chutney or you can have a hot sauce dip too.

Makes 24

Ingredients:

8oz Salt cod soaked overnight in cold water and discard
3 Medium potatoes peeled and diced
1 Large tomato peeled and chopped
1 Medium onion finely chopped
1 Garlic clove minced
1 tsp **Tan Rosie's Garlic & pepper Sauce (HOT)**
1 Cup plain flour
½ tsp Freshly grated nutmeg
Salt & Black Pepper
1 Egg beaten
1 tbsp Fish sauce
½ Green pepper chopped

Method:

1. Immerse pre-soaked salt cod in boiling water for 15 minutes.
2. Remove bones and skin from fish and flake.
3. Cook potatoes until tender.
4. Drain the potatoes and mash together with flaked fish until well combined.
5. In a food processor, place tomato, green peppers, onion, garlic, hot sauce, nutmeg, flour and salt and black pepper, 1 tbsp fish sauce and blend for a few seconds.
6. Pour sauce over mashed cod and potato mixture and combine all ingredients well.
7. Add beaten egg and mix together. The mixture should be firm enough to form balls about the size of a walnut.
8. Fry balls in hot deep fat until golden brown.

Tip:

Smoked salmon or smoked haddock can be substituted for salt cod.

Stuffed Plantains
with Spinach

There are a variety of ways to cook plantains and this recipe is a fun and tasty option. It's great as a starter dish for your dinner party and its tasty with a little hot sauce as a dip.

Serves 4

Ingredients:
2 Large ripe plantains
2 tbsp Butter
2 tbsp Onions finely chopped
450g Fresh spinach chopped
2 Garlic cloves minced
1 Egg beaten
¼ tsp grated nutmeg
Salt & Black Pepper to taste
Plain flour for dusting
Oil for frying
1 tsp **Tan Rosie's Garlic & Pepper Sauce (HOT)**

Method:
1. Slice each plantain into four pieces length-ways.
2. Heat a little oil in a large frying pan and fry plantain on both sides until golden brown, but just under cooked
3. Place on kitchen paper to drain.
4. In a separate pan, place butter and sauté onions and garlic for 3 minutes until onions are soft.
5. Add spinach and nutmeg, **Tan Rosie's Garlic & Pepper Sauce (HOT)** with salt and pepper to taste.
6. Cover and cook for 5 minutes or so, until the spinach has wilted.
7. When spinach mixture is cool, place in strainer to press out excess liquid.
8. Form plantain into rings and secure with a cocktail stick.
9. Pack each plantain ring with the cooked spinach mixture.
10. In two plates place beaten egg and flour.
11. Place oil in frying pan on a medium heat.
12. Dip plantain rounds in egg, then dust with flour.
13. Shallow fry on both sides for 2 minutes until golden brown.
14. Drain on kitchen paper and serve.

Ackee & Salt Fish
with Fried Dumplings

Ackee and Salt Fish is a very famous and traditional Jamaican dish. It's a great crowd-pleaser, very colourful and tastes fantastic.

Serves 6

Ackee Ingredients:
450g Salt cod
1 Lemon
1oz Butter
2 tbsp Olive oil
1 Onion minced
2 Garlic cloves minced
8oz Tomatoes skinned & chopped
1 Small scotch bonnet pepper, de seeded and chopped
1 tbsp Freshly chopped thyme
4 Spring onions chopped
¼ tsp Black pepper
1 Can Ackee, drained

Dumplings Ingredients:
2 Cups Self raising flour
1tsp Salt
1oz Butter
Water to make firm dough
Oil for frying

Ackee Method:
1. Place cod in a bowl of cold water in juice of lemon and soak for 24 hours. Change water & lemon 2-3 times to remove saltiness.
2. After 24 hours, remove and drain water. Place in a bowl, add boiling water and leave to steep for 15 minutes.
3. Drain, remove, skin and de-bone the fish, then flake.
4. In a saucepan, place oil and butter on a medium heat, gently sauté onions and garlic for 5 minutes without browning.
5. Add tomatoes, scotch bonnet peppers and continue to sauté for 3-5 minutes.
6. Add salt fish, thyme, spring onions and simmer for 5 minutes and adjust seasoning.
7. Add drained ackee and allow this to warm through, but not boil. Then serve with fried dumplings.

Dumplings Method:
1. Place all dry ingredients in a bowl and mix to a film dough with water. Then leave to rest for 15 minutes.
2. Form into small balls, place oil in a frying pan and bring up to medium heat
3. Add dumplings and fry until golden brown and cooked through, turning as required to prevent burning.
4. When cooked, remove and drain and serve with salt fish and ackee.

Bajan Cou Cou with Fried Snapper & Pepper Sauce

This recipe is a twist on the traditional Barbadian dish "Cou Cou and Flying Fish." "Cou Cou" is the Bajan term for Polenta. You can use any kind of firm fish for this particular dish such as cod, haddock or salmon.

Serves 6

Cou Cou Ingredients:
8oz Polenta medium
8oz Okra trimmed and cut into slices
Salt & black pepper
1 Cup Coconut milk
2 Cups Vegetable stock
3 tbsp Butter

Fried Snapper Ingredients:
6 Red snapper fillets
1 Cup vegetable oil
½ tsp Salt
½ tsp Black Pepper
1 Cup plain flour
Juice of 1 lime or lemon
Lemon or lime slice for garnish

Cou Cou Method:
1. In a deep saucepan, place vegetable stock and bring to the boil.
2. Add okras and cook for 10 minutes.
3. Remove okras and put to one side.
4. Add coconut milk to saucepan with vegetable stock from cooked okras and bring to boil.
5. Remove half the liquid from saucepan and whisk in polenta or cornmeal.
6. Continue to add liquid as polenta thickens.
7. Return the okra to polenta mixture and stir together.
8. Add remaining vegetable liquid to form a soft consistency and cook for 5 minutes stirring to prevent sticking.
9. Add butter, stir and serve.

Fried Snapper Method:
1. Rinse red snapper fillets in juice of lime or lemon.
2. Cut fillets into goujons or strips.
3. Pat dry with kitchen paper.
4. In a plastic bag, place flour, salt and pepper and shake to mix thoroughly.
5. Add strips of fish and shake, then remove from flour mix.
6. Place frying pan on medium heat and add oil.
7. When oil is hot, fry fish strips until lightly golden brown.
8. Remove with slotted spoon onto kitchen paper to absorb excess oil and serve with cou cou.

Pepper Sauce Method:
See page 23 for sauce ingredients and method.

Mains

Curry Mutton

Curry mutton is one of our favourite dishes from the Caribbean. We always have this dish at family parties and get togethers of all kinds. Usually at parties, this is served towards the end of the night with roti, plain rice or rice and peas.

Serves 6

Ingredients:

1 kg Mutton diced with any gristle and fat removed
1 Large onion chopped
3 Cloves Garlic minced
2oz **Tan Rosie's Caribbean Style Curry Powder**
Few sprigs fresh thyme
2 Bay leaves
1 tsp Ground allspice
½ tsp Ground cloves
¼ Cup Vegetable oil
¼ Cup Butter
1 Scotch bonnet pepper left whole
2 Cups vegetable stock, lamb stock or water
1 Cup coconut milk
1 tsp Salt
1 tsp Black pepper

Method:

1. In a non metallic bowl place mutton, onions, garlic, thyme, curry powder, allspice, cloves, bay leaves and oil.
2. Mix all ingredients together well. Cover bowl and marinade for 2 to 3 hours or overnight in fridge.
3. In large frying pan place butter with a little oil, allow to melt on medium heat.
4. Add mutton to frying pan and fry on medium heat for about 10 to 15 minutes stirring frequently until brown.
5. Add stock, coconut milk and scotch bonnet pepper, bring to the boil. Lower heat and simmer gently for 90 minutes or until meat is tender.
6. For a thickened sauce increase heat for the last 10 minutes stirring occasionally without breaking up meat pieces.
7. Serve with Roti or boiled rice.

Tip:

Lamb, goat, chicken or beef can be used instead of mutton in this recipe.

Pollo Borracho
(Drunken Chicken)

Pollo Borracho is a typical Cuban supper dish. Spanish olives, white wine and white rum are combined to create a great tasting chicken dish. Serve with saffron rice (Arroz Amarillo Page 71) for an authentic Cuban meal.

Serves 6

Ingredients:

12 Chicken thighs skin removed
4 Cloves garlic minced
1 Large onion medium sliced
2 Bay leaves
1 Cup dry white wine
½ Cup white rum
1 Cup unpitted large green olives, drained
¼ Cup Spanish olive oil
1 tsp dried oregano
Sea salt and freshly ground black pepper to taste
Juice of 1 lime or lemon

Method:

1. With the juice of lemon or lime, wash chicken thighs. Pat dry using kitchen paper towels.
2. Place chicken in bowl. Massage salt, pepper and oregano into chicken thighs. Leave to marinade for 3 hours or overnight in the fridge.
3. In large heavy bottomed frying pan, heat olive oil over medium heat. Brown chicken thighs on either side, a light brown colour should be aimed for.
4. Remove browned chicken thighs from pan and set aside.
5. Reduce heat under pan to low add onions and garlic, cook until tender without colouring. This should take about 8 to 10 minutes.
6. Add bay leaves, wine, rum and olives bring to the boil.
7. Return chicken thighs to pan, cover and cook for 45 to 50 minutes.
8. Remove bay leaves. Serve with saffron rice (Arroz Amarillo page 71).

Breadfruit Oildown

Oildown is Grenada's national dish . It's essentially a 1-pot dish with salted or preserved meats and a variety of vegetables. It's very easy to prepare and delicious to eat!

Serves 6

Ingredients:

½ lb smoked ham or gammon diced
1 tbsp olive oil
1 Large onion chopped
2 Cloves garlic minced
1 Red pepper diced
½ Scotch bonnet pepper de seeded, and stem removed and finely chopped
1 Bunch spring onions chopped
1 tbsp fresh thyme
4 Cups coconut milk
500g Spinach or callaloo chopped
1 Large breadfruit peeled and cut into 2" pieces
Sea salt and black pepper to taste
50g butter

Method:

1. Heat oil in a saucepan, sauté onions, for 5 minutes until soft.
2. Add peppers, garlic, spring onions, ham and thyme continue to sauté for a further 5 minutes, stirring at times
3. Add coconut milk and breadfruit and bring to the boil.
4. Reduce heat and simmer 30 minutes.
5. Add spinach and butter allow to wilt down for 5 minutes
6. Add salt and pepper to taste.

Geera Pork

Geera Pork is a traditional Trinidadian dish. It's an Indian influenced dish, which is usually served with Hops bread (a traditional Trinidadian bread).

Serves 4 - 6

Ingredients:
1 ½ lbs Pork cubed
1 tbsp Geera (cumin), roasted and ground
4 Cloves garlic minced
1 Large onion finely chopped
1 tbsp Fresh coriander chopped
1 Red pepper diced
1 Scotch bonnet pepper
6 Spring onions chopped
1 tbsp fresh thyme
2 Cups vegetable stock/water
Salt and pepper to taste
Juice of 1 lime or lemon
2 tbsp vegetable oil
1 tbsp butter

Method:
1. Wash pork with the juice of lime or lemon. Pat dry with kitchen paper.
2. Place pork in a bowl, add geera, salt and pepper, thyme, mix well and leave to marinade for 2 hours or overnight if possible.
3. In a frying pan place oil and butter on medium heat.
4. Add onion, sauté for 5 minutes until soft and tender and golden brown.
5. Add garlic and spring onions, stirring and cooking for 1 minute.
6. Add pork to onion mixture, continue to sauté stirring to allow pork to seal and brown all over.
7. Add red pepper, whole scotch bonnet pepper, coriander and water, bring to boil and simmer for 50 minutes until pork is tender.
8. Remove scotch bonnet pepper and discard.
9. Allow pork mixture liquid to reduce to a thick consistency and remove from heat.

Bajan Beef Stew

We served this classic Barbadian (Bajan) stew with coconut rice on our Bajan supper club night. The beef was very tender and juicy with a rich sauce and complimented the coconut rice (page 74). You can also eat this dish with your favourite chutney for extra pizzazz!

Serves 6 - 8

Ingredients:

2 lbs beef, cubed
1 Large onion finely chopped
4 Garlic cloves finely minced
1 tbsp vegetable oil
1 tbsp Butter
½ tsp ground allspice
½ tsp ground cloves
1 tsp **Tan Rosie's Garlic & Pepper Sauce (HOT)**
2 Sticks celery diced
½ lb carrots diced
1 tsp Fresh thyme
1 Bay leaf
½ tsp Dried oregano
1 Large beetroot diced
4 Cups beef stock/ vegetable stock
Salt and ground black pepper to taste
1 tsp Worcestershire sauce
1 tsp gravy browning
1 tbsp Butter and flour mixed to a paste
1 Beef cube

Method:

1. Wash beef and dry with paper towel.
2. Place beef in bowl with onions, garlic, pepper sauce, allspice, cloves, herbs, Worcestershire sauce, celery and beef cube.
3. Mix well and leave to marinate for at least 3 hours or overnight in the fridge.
4. In a frying pan place oil, bring to heat add oil and sauté marinated beef for about 10 minutes, turning to brown evenly.
5. Add stock and gravy browning and bay leaf bring to the boil.
6. Reduce heat and simmer on low heat for 1 hour or until beef is tender.
7. Add flour and butter paste to beef stew to thicken. Continue to stir until blended.
8. Add vegetables salt and pepper to taste, continue to cook until vegetables are tender for about 15 to 20 minutes.

Tip:

Stew can be cooked in a covered casserole in oven on medium heat for 1 ½ hours. For the last ½ hour of cooking place casserole on hob to reduce sauce to a thick consistency.

Spicy Slow Roast Mutton

Slow roasted meats are a common favourite in our home and this recipe is no exception. Caribbean spices such as allspice and cloves really makes mutton come alive.

Serves 8 - 10

Ingredients:

1 Shoulder or leg of Mutton
2 Onions chopped
4 Cloves garlic
3 Scotch bonnet peppers de seeded and chopped
1 tbsp fresh thyme
½ Cup brown sugar
1 Bunch spring onions chopped
1 tsp ground allspice
1 tsp ground cloves
1 tsp freshly grated nutmeg
¼ Cup soya sauce
¼ Cup olive oil
1 tsp sea salt
Juice of 2 limes or lemons

Method:

1. In large bowl place mutton. Make some slashes in meat.
2. Place all other ingredients in food processor and blend together.
3. Rub marinade into meat, ensuring all marinade gets well into slashed areas. Leave to marinade for up to 48 hours in the fridge.
4. Remove from fridge and leave to reach room temperature.
5. Preheat oven to high.
6. Place mutton in roasting pan, covered with foil roast for 20 minutes on high.
7. Reduce heat low and slow roast for 6 hours until meat is falling off bone.
8. For the last 45 minutes remove foil covering and baste meat with pan juices.
9. Remove from heat/oven and leave to rest, covered before pulling apart and serving.

Rice & Peas Chicken Pelau

This is another traditional dish from Carriacou, Grenada that's got my own twist. It's a very hearty meal and has been enjoyed by my family and friends for many years.

Serves 4

Ingredients:
250gm Easy Cook Rice
40gm **'Tan Rosie's Jerk Rub'**
250gm Pigeon Peas (or tinned variety) soaked overnight
4 Chicken thighs (skinned)
1 Medium Onion (minced)
2 Garlic cloves (diced)
½ Tin Coconut Milk
100gm Smoked Bacon or Salt Pork/Beef
1 Scotch Bonnet Pepper
Black Pepper to taste
2 tsp Fresh Thyme
2 tsp Vegetable Stock
500ml Water
Salad Leaves for serving

Method:
1. Massage Jerk Rub into chicken and leave overnight in fridge
2. Heat oil in a pan, add chicken then brown
3. Add bacon, onions & cook for 5 mins
4. Add coconut milk, peas, thyme, water, scotch bonnet pepper, stock and bring to boil, then simmer for 15mins on low heat
5. Add rice and stir, bring to boil, add lid and simmer for 15mins on low heat, then serve with a fresh salad

Tip:
1. Make sure you remove scotch bonnet pepper before serving!
2. If using dried peas, soak overnight and cook to tender for 40 minutes.

Coo Coo & Baked Goat Fish

Coo Coo (Polenta) is Carriacou's National Dish and Goat fish is also a traditional Carriacouan fish. This dish has been eaten by my family for many years, it's filling and very tasty.

Serves 6

Coo Coo Ingredients:
200gm Polenta/Corn Meal
1 ltr Water
30ml Vegetable Oil and Butter
1 tbsp Salt or Vegetable stock powder
Black Pepper to taste
3 Spring Onions
1 Tin coconut milk

Okra Ingredients:
250gm Okras (sliced)
Salt & Black Pepper to taste
250ml Water
1 sml Spring Onions (diced)

Goat Fish Ingredients:
3 Goat Fishes
1 tbsp **'Tan Rosie's Garlic & Pepper Sauce (HOT)'**
1 tbsp Fish Sauce
½ Lemon (Juice)
Salt & Black Pepper to taste
1 tbsp Fresh Thyme

Coo Coo method:
1. Add oil, butter and spring onions in pan then sauté for 1 minute.
2. Add water, coconut milk, vegetable stock and bring to boil.
3. Whisk polenta into boiling liquid until thick paste (if too thick add water) then cook for 5 minutes.
4. Butter a dish then pour into bowl.

Okra method:
1. Remove head & tail of okra.
2. Add oil to pan, add onions and fry for 5 minutes until softened.
3. Add okras, quartered tomatoes, water, salt & pepper.
4. Bring to boil and simmer for 10 mins, then serve.

Goat Fish method:
1. Clean & gut fish.
2. Add to slashes to either side of fish.
3. Place all other ingredients into a bowl with fish and leave to marinade for ½ hour.
4. Remove fish, then shallow fry for 12 mins either side.
5. Then place in baking dish, cover then bake for 5 minutes on medium heat, then serve.

Tip:
1. Always whisk the polenta, as this prevents lumps occurring.
2. You can also use salmon or haddock as an alternative to Goat fish.

Chicken Roti

Chicken Roti is a fantastic street food dish served in many parts of the Caribbean. I've used a Paratha roti recipe which originates from India via Trinidad. It's great for lunch when you are at Paradise beach in Hillsborough town, Carriacou!

Serves 6

Chicken Curry Ingredients:

500gm Boned Chicken Thighs (Cubed).
40gm **'Tan Rosie Caribbean Style Curry Powder'**
1 tbsp Vegetable Oil
1 Scotch Bonnet Pepper
1 medium Potato (Cubed)
200ml Coconut Milk
1 Large Onion (Minced)
2 Garlic Cloves (Minced)
1 tsp Salt & Black Pepper
100 ml Water

Roti Ingredients:

500gm Flour
1 tbsp Baking Powder
1 tsp Salt
50gm Ghee
Water (enough to form soft dough)

To make the Chicken Curry:

1. Cut boned chicken thigh into cubes.
2. Massage curry powder into chicken & leave overnight.
3. Heat oil in a pan, then add onions & sauté for 5 mins until golden brown.
4. Add minced garlic & sauté for 1 minute.
5. Add seasoned chicken and fry until brown.
6. Add coconut milk, water, potato, salt, pepper & scotch bonnet pepper and cover pot and bring to boil & simmer for 40 mins.
7. Remove cover and reduce liquid until thickened.
8. Remove scotch bonnet pepper and serve.

To Make Roti:

1. Add flour, salt & baking powder into a bowl.
2. Add some water (enough to form a soft pliable dough) then mix for 5 mins.
3. Turn out onto floured surface & knead until smooth – cover & leave for 15mins.
4. Melt ghee in pan and add some flour to make a paste, then cut dough into 4 portions and make round balls and roll out into 10" disc.
5. Brush ghee paste onto disc and cut from centre of disc to outer edge and roll together to form a cone shape.
6. Place the cone on surface, push the peak down so it is flat and roll out into 12" diameter disc (the cone shape makes the layers).
7. Place on a hot tawa or gridle stone and cook for 1 min – turn and brush with ghee and repeat until brown specs appear.
9. Remove and cover with warm towel – then repeat until all the dough is cooked.

Tip:

Make sure you have a plate and warm towel ready for the rotis. Plus, it's important to leave the chicken to marinade for at least 2 hours or overnight.

Tan Rosie's Jerk Chicken

This is such an easy way to make jerk chicken if you are in a hurry. Our Jerk Rub seasoning is medium heat, but you can add extra heat if needed. Try cooking the jerk chicken on the barbecue for an even tastier flavour!

Serves 4

Ingredients:
40gm **'Tan Rosie's Jerk Rub'**
Chicken Portions x4
Olive Oil

Method:
1. Place chicken pieces in bowl.
2. Rub with olive oil.
3. Massage 2 tablespoons of **Tan Rosie's Jerk Rub** into meat.
4. Leave to rest for 2 hours or preferably overnight.
5. Roast in oven for 40mins on medium heat.
6. Serve with chips or baked potatoes and a green salad. This also tastes great with **'Tan Rosie's Garlic & Pepper Sauce(HOT)'** for extra heat!

Vegetarian Dishes

Vegetarian Dishes
Channa Dhal
(Chick Pea & Potato Curry)

Channa dhal is another traditional Trinidadian dish with influences from India.
This is a superb vegetarian dish which can be eaten with plain rice, "Buss Up
Shut" roti (page 50) and your favourite chutney.

Serves 6

Ingredients:
2 Cups chick peas soaked overnight and cooked
1 lb Potatoes diced
1 Large onion diced
2 Garlic cloves minced
1 Scotch bonnet pepper
1 tbsp Olive
1 tbsp Butter
1 tbsp Fresh coriander
50g **Tan Rosie Caribbean Style Curry Powder**
2 Cups Water/vegetable stock
1 Cup coconut milk
Salt and black pepper to taste
½ Cup chopped tomato

Method:
1. Place oil and butter in saucepan on medium heat.
2. Add onions to pan, sauté for 5 to 10 minutes, stirring to allow even cooking until slightly brown and soft.
3. Add garlic, cook for 1 minute stirring .
4. Add **Tan Rosie's Caribbean Style Curry Powder** to pan, stirring and cooking for 1 minute
5. Add chopped tomato, chick peas, potatoes, stock, coconut milk, herbs, and stir and bring to the boil.
6. Reduce heat and simmer for 20 minutes and cover until vegetables are tender.
7. Remove cover, allow liquid to reduce down to a thick consistency, for about 5 minutes depending on amount of liquor in pan
8. Serve with boiled basmati or roti garnished with fresh coriander leaves.

Vegetarian Dishes
Frijoles Negros & Bonito Bake
(Black Bean & Sweet Potato Bake)

Black Beans are used widely in Cuban food. This is a great recipe we came up with to utilize this tasty pulse. It's very comforting and moreish, so enjoy!

Serves 6

Ingredients For Black Bean Base/Stew:
2 Cups black beans cooked,
1 Cup vegetable stock or 1 cup of reserved liquor from boiled beans
1 Large onion finely chopped
2 Cloves garlic minced
1 tbsp olive oil
1 tbsp butter
1 tsp dried oregano
1 tsp **Tan Rosie's Garlic & Pepper Sauce (HOT)**
Sea salt and black pepper to taste

Ingredients For Sweet Potato Topping:
2lbs sweet potatoes
200g Grated mature cheddar cheese
1 tbsp butter
½ Cup double cream
100g grated mature cheese for sprinkling on top
Salt & black pepper to taste

Method For Black Bean Base:
1. In saucepan heat olive oil and butter over medium heat.
2. Add onions fry for 5 minutes until soft and golden brown.
3. Add garlic and oregano, stir and cook for further 1 minute.
4. Add Beans, stock/liquor, hot sauce and bring to the boil.
5. Turn heat down to low, cover pan and cook for 15 minutes.
6. Season to taste with salt and pepper.
7. In a baking dish, place bean mixture and allow to cool before adding sweet potato topping.

Method For Sweet Potato Topping:
1. Peel and boil sweet potato until tender in salted water.
2. Drain potato and mash, a potato ricer can be used which would give a smoother outcome
3. Add butter, cheese, double cream salt and pepper and blend thoroughly.
4. Place sweet potato topping on to black bean base and smoothed over.
5. Sprinkle over cheese
6. Bake in medium heat at gas mark 7 for 30 to 35 minutes until golden brown.

Caribbean Style Nut Roast

This recipe is our twist on the humble nut roast, Caribbean style! It's perfect for Christmas lunch or for a special occasion with friends. We made this with an accompaniment of our own **Tan Rosie's Garlic & Pepper Sauce (HOT)**. It just gives an extra hit of heat which peps up the dish. Try it!

Serves 6

Ingredients:

150g Cashew nuts
150g Brazil nuts
250g Chestnuts
1 Cup fresh bread crumbs
1 Large onion chopped
2 Garlic cloves minced
½ Cup dried cranberries
1 tbsp Fresh thyme
1 tbsp Parsley chopped
2 Eggs beaten
1 Vegetable stock cube crushed
Pinch nutmeg
¼ tsp Allspice
1 tsp **Tan Rosie's Garlic & Pepper Sauce (HOT)**
¼ tsp sea salt
¼ teaspoon Black pepper
1 tbsp Olive oil
1 tbsp Butter

Method:

1. Grease loaf tin with butter.
2. Preheat oven to gas mark 7 or medium heat.
3. Place Brazil, cashew and chestnuts in food processor and coarsely ground.
4. Place nut mix in bowl.
5. Place oil and butter in frying pan on medium heat, add chopped onions and fry until golden brown, about 5 minutes.
6. Add garlic to onion and cook for 1 minute.
7. Remove from heat and cool.
8. Add cooled onion and garlic to nut mix and combine all other ingredients together.
9. Place nut roast in loaf tin, dot top of nut roast with butter.
10. Place nut roast in oven.
11. Bake for 40 to 45 minutes until top is golden brown.

Spicy Aubergine & Sweet Potato Bake

As you can see from this picture it went down really well at our supper club night! It can also be eaten as a side dish or you can add minced beef or lamb for your meat-eating guests.

Serves 6

Aubergine Ingredients:

2 Large Aubergines, sliced

500g tomatoes peeled and chopped

1 Large onion chopped

2 Garlic cloves minced

1 tsp Oregano

1 tbsp Fresh basil leaves

¼ tsp salt

¼ tsp black pepper

2 tsp sugar

1 tbsp Tomato paste

2 tbsp olive oil

2 tbsp butter

1 tsp **Tan Rosie's Garlic & Pepper Sauce (HOT)**

Sweet Potato Mash Ingredients:

2 Cups sweet potato cooked

1 tbsp butter

¼ Cup double cream

250g grated mature cheddar

Salt and pepper to taste

Method:
1. Grill aubergine slices until golden brown. Set to one side.

For tomato sauce:
1. In frying pan put oil and butter on medium heat.
2. Place onions in pan and cook for 5 minutes until soft and golden brown.
3. Add garlic, cook for further 1 minute.
4. Add basil, chopped tomato, herbs, sugar, salt and pepper, hot sauce to onion mix and bring to the boil.
5. Reduce heat and simmer for 20 minutes.
6. Add tomato paste, stir and cook down for 5 minutes.
7. Remove from heat and cool.

For sweet potato mash:
1. Combine all ingredients to form sweet potato topping. Set aside
2. Grease casserole dish with some butter.
3. Place a layer of aubergine in dish.
4. Spoon some of the tomato sauce over aubergine.
5. Repeat layering process until all aubergines is used up.
6. Finish with the Sweet Potato mash evenly spread.
7. Bake in oven for 45 minutes in preheated oven at gas mark 7.

Vegetarian Dishes
Ital Stew

Ital stew is a famous Jamaican Rastafarian dish. "Ital" is taken from the word "vital." The Rastafarian diet is vegan, so eating pure and natural vegetables and pulses are essential to their religion. It's a colourful and hearty stew, perfect as a starter or main dish.

Serves 6

Ingredients:
1 Cup cooked kidney beans
1 Large onion chopped
4 Spring onions chopped
3 Cloves garlic minced
1 Cup sweet potato diced
1 Cup yam diced
1 Cup cassava diced
2 Large carrots diced
2 Sticks celery diced
1 Medium white potato diced
2 tbsp Olive oil
1 tbsp butter
½ Cup chopped tomato
4 Sprigs of thyme
4 Cups coconut milk
1 Cup vegetable stock
¼ tsp Allspice
¼ tsp Cinnamon
250g Spinach chopped
1 Scotch bonnet pepper
Salt and black pepper to taste
Pinch of saffron

Dumpling Ingredients:
1 Cup whole wheat flour
Pinch salt and black pepper
1 tsp sugar
Knob of butter
Water to mix

Method:
1. Place olive oil and butter in saucepan and place on medium heat.
2. Place onions in saucepan and cook for 5 minutes until golden brown and soft.
3. Add garlic, cook for 1 minute.
4. Add carrots, celery and continue to cook for further 3 minutes
5. Add chopped tomato, allspice, cinnamon, saffron, thyme and scotch bonnet pepper, stir.
6. Add coconut milk, kidney beans, vegetable stock, bring to the boil cover pan and simmer for 15 minutes.
7. After 15 minutes, add vegetables, bring back to boil.
8. Add dumplings, continue cooking until vegetables are tender and dumplings are cooked.
9. Add spinach, spring onions and cook for further 5 minutes.

Dumplings Method:
1. Mix all ingredients together to firm stiff dough.
2. Leave to rest for 10 minutes.
3. Make small round balls.
4. Add to ital stew as directed above.

Macaroni Pie

Every Caribbean household eats macaroni pie! This is a staple dish in every home across all the islands. It's a comforting, delicious dish which we eat with anything from curry chicken, fried chicken and much more.

Serves 6

Ingredients:
250g Macaroni
375g Mature cheddar grated
1 Large onion finely chopped
1 tbsp Olive oil
1 tbsp Butter
2 Cups Milk
1 tsp Mustard powder
Pinch grated nutmeg
Sea salt and black pepper to taste
2 Eggs beaten
1 tsp **Tan Rosie's Garlic & Pepper Sauce (HOT)**
1 Medium plum tomato sliced for garnish
For Cheese and bread crumb topping:
150g Fresh bread crumbs
100g Grated mature cheddar cheese
1 tbsp Butter
Mix all the ingredient together to make topping

Method:
1. Grease casserole or pie dish.
2. Preheat oven to gas mark 7.
3. Cook macaroni in salted boiling water for 10 minutes, macaroni need to be al dente' as it will be further cooked in the pie.
4. Drain return to pan and set aside.
5. Mixing in some olive oil into pasta will prevent it from sticking while the other stages are being done.
6. In frying pan add olive oil and butter, fry onions until golden brown for about 5 to 8 minutes.
7. Add fried onions and other ingredients to macaroni and mix thoroughly.
8. Place mixture in greased pie dish, spread cheesy topping over pie.
9. Garnish with tomato slices.
10. Bake in oven for 35 to 40 minutes or until golden brown.

Side Dishes

Traditional Rice & Peas

Rice and peas is a very traditional dish in the Caribbean. Each region has its own twist on the recipe. Jamaicans tend to use kidney beans, but my family in Carriacou Grenada have always used pigeon peas or gungo peas. It's a timeless recipe that I hope you'll enjoy making.

Serves 6

Ingredients:
2 Cups Gungo peas
1 ½ Cups long grain easy cook rice
3 Cups coconut milk
1 tbsp Fresh thyme
1 Scotch bonnet pepper
1 Large onion finely chopped
2 Garlic cloves minced
1 tbsp Olive oil
1 tbsp Butter
Salt and black pepper to taste
1 Vegetable stock cube
1 Bay leaf
1 Clove garlic
6 Whole cloves

Method:
1. Soak gungo peas in cold water overnight.
2. Drain water from peas and discard water.
3. In saucepan place drained peas with cold water, 1 garlic clove, bay leaf, and whole cloves.
4. Bring pan to boil, reduce heat and simmer for 40 to 45 minutes until peas are tender
5. Next, place frying pan on medium heat, add olive oil, butter and onions and sauté for 5 minutes.
6. Add garlic and thyme, fry for a further 1 minute.
7. Remove from heat and add onion mixture to peas, add coconut milk, scotch bonnet pepper and bring to the boil.
8. Add rice, vegetable stock cube, salt and pepper to taste.
9. Stir ingredients, bring to boil and cover pan, and reduce heat to low.
10. Allow to cook until all liquid is absorbed and rice is tender for about 20 minutes.
11. Remove from heat and allow to rest covered for 10 minutes before serving.

Side Dishes
Fried Plantains

Fried plantains are a superb side dish for any Caribbean meal. Make sure the plantains are ripe, as they will taste sweeter and juicer!

Serves 6

Ingredients:
4 Ripe plantains
Oil for frying
Salt and Black pepper

Method:
1. Peel plantains
2. Divide each plantain into 2 crossways, then each portion into 2 lengthways.
3. In frying pan, heat oil to medium hot.
4. Place plantains in hot oil, fry until golden brown on each side.
5. Remove from oil with slotted spoon, place onto absorbent kitchen paper.
6. Sprinkle with salt and pepper and serve.

Arroz Amarillo
(Yellow Rice)

Arroz amarillo is a classic Cuban side dish made with their traditional Sofrito sauce. We served this with Pollo Borracho (Drunken Chicken) page 40. This rice dish has a subtle flavour which really goes well with chicken or lamb dishes.

Serves 6

Ingredients for the Sofrito (tomato sauce with peppers and sherry):

¼ Cup extra virgin olive oil
3 Cloves garlic minced
1 Medium onion, minced
1 Green pepper, de seeded and chopped finely
1 Cup tomato pasata or drained chopped tomatoes
¼ Cup dry sherry
¼ Cup Diced red peppers or chopped drained pimentos
1 Bay leaf
2 tsp **Tan Rosie's Garlic & Pepper Sauce (HOT)**

Ingredients for Rice:

2 Cups long grain easy cook rice
4 Cups water
2 tsp sea salt
1 pinch of saffron soaked in warm water
Pinch freshly grated black pepper.

Method:

1. In saucepan over medium heat, add olive oil and heat.
2. Add garlic, onions, peppers and cook for 10 minutes until tender.
3. Add tomatoes, sherry and bay leaf then continue cooking for 10 minutes on low heat.
4. Next add water, salt, rice and soaked saffron, stir and bring to the boil.
5. Reduce heat, cover and cook for 15 minutes until all liquid is absorbed.
6. Fork through to fluff rice, cover and let it rest for another 10 minutes before serving.

Sweet Potato Mash

This is a great alternative to regular mash. You can serve this mash with a curry chicken, lamb or beef.

Serves 6

Ingredients:
1lb Sweet potato
1tbsp Butter
½ Cup double cream
1tsp Salt and pepper
2 Stalks spring onions finely chopped for garnish

Method:
1. Peel and cube sweet potato.
2. Place saucepan with water on heat. Add salt and sweet potato and bring to boil.
3. Reduce heat and simmer for 10 to 15 minutes.
4. Remove from heat and drain off water.
5. Return pan to heat for 1 minute to allow all water to evaporate.
6. Remove pan from heat, add butter, cream, salt and pepper to taste and mash all ingredients together to a smooth consistency.
7. A potato can be used to achieve this or a potato masher will do as well.
8. Serve with spring onion to garnish.

Tip:
White sweet potato is ideal for this mash. Available at any Asian supermarket/grocer.

Crushed Yams

This crushed yams recipe uses double cream to give a rich velvety taste. It tastes great with fish, or meat dishes with a rich sauce.

Serves 4

Ingredients:
1lb Yams
1tbsp Butter
1 tbsp Olive oil
1 tsp Salt
1 Large onion finely minced
1 Garlic clove minced
¼ Cup double cream
1 tbsp Chopped parsley

Method:
1. Peel yams and dice.
2. Place yams in saucepan with water and salt on heat. Bring to boil, reduce heat and simmer for 10 minutes or until yam is tender.
3. Remove from heat, drain water and discard. Cover yams and set aside.
4. Place oil and butter in a frying pan on medium heat.
5. Add onion, fry for 5 minutes, stirring until golden brown.
6. Add garlic and fry for a further 1 minute.
7. Add onion and garlic mixture to yam with double cream.
8. Crush mixture together.
9. Sprinkle with parsley and serve.

Coconut Rice

We served this coconut rice dish at our Bajan Supper Club night with a Beef stew. It's a popular side dish which can be eaten with a variety of main dishes.

Serves 6

Ingredients:
1 ½ Cups Basmati rice
2 Cups Coconut milk
1 Cup Vegetable stock
1 Medium onion minced
1 tbsp Olive oil
1 tbsp Butter
1 tsp salt
Black pepper
Chopped parsley for garnish

Method:
1. Soak basmati rice in cold water for 30 minutes, then drain.
2. In saucepan, add oil and butter and place on medium heat, fry for 5 minutes, stirring occasionally until golden brown.
3. Add drained rice to onions, stirring to allow rice to be covered with the mixture.
4. Add vegetable stock, coconut milk, salt and pepper to taste, stir, bring to boil.
5. Cover pan, reduce heat to simmer, cook for 10 minutes until liquid is absorbed.
6. Turn off heat and leave covered for another 15 minutes.
7. Garnish with parsley and serve.

Tip:
Any left over rice can used in a stir fry the next day.

Baked Plantains in Orange Juice

This is one of my favourite recipes for plantains. At our supper club, I like to experiment with traditional Caribbean ingredients and this side dish is a crowd pleaser!

Serves 8

Ingredients:
4 Ripe plantains
Rind and juice of 1 orange
Salt and pepper to taste
1 tbsp Butter
1 tbsp Chopped spring onions

Method:
1. Grease baking dish with some butter.
2. Preheat oven to medium heat gas mark 7.
3. Peel plantains, cut each into 2 crossways and each portion into 2 lengthways.
4. Arrange sliced plantains in greased dish, sprinkle with rind of orange and juice, salt and pepper and dot with butter.
5. Cover with foil securely and bake in oven for 25 to 30 minutes.
6. Remove from oven sprinkle with spring onions and serve.

Roasted Sweet Potatoes

This is a really easy recipe to try if you want roast potatoes with a twist!

Serves 6

Ingredients:

2 lbs Sweet potato, peeled and cut into chunks
3 Shallots sliced thickly
2 Cloves garlic sliced
3 Sprigs of fresh thyme
2 tbsp olive oil
1 tbsp butter
1 tsp Sea salt
Black pepper

Method:

1. Preheat oven to gas mark 7.
2. Place all ingredients into a large freezer bag, seal and mix together.
3. Empty ingredients from freezer bag into roasting tin, discard freezer bag.
4. Place in roasting in. Roast for 45 minutes until golden brown, turning occasionally.
5. Remove from oven, discard thyme sprigs and serve while hot.

Plantain Dumplings

I came up with this recipe to use leftover ripe plantains. It tastes fantastic combined with a dumpling mixture. You can add these dumplings to stews or eat them as a side dish. Enjoy them!

Serves 8

Ingredients:
1 Very ripe plantain, peeled and mashed
1 Cup self raising flour
½ tsp Salt
½ tsp black pepper
1 Knob of butter
Water to mix
Olive oil for garnish

Method:
1. Place all ingredients in a mixing bowl.
2. Mix thoroughly.
3. Add some water and mix to form firm dough.
4. Cover and allow to rest for 15 minutes.
5. In a saucepan water and bring to boil on medium heat.
6. Roll out dough into small balls and drop into the boiling salted water, cover and boil on reduced heat for 10 minutes or until dumplings are cooked through.
7. When cooked, the dumplings will rise to the top of the liquid.
8. Remove dumplings from pan, sprinkle with olive oil and serve.

Carrot & Herb Loaf

Our carrot and herb loaf can be eaten as part of a starter or as a snack with cheese and a dash of **Tan Rosie's Garlic & Pepper Sauce (HOT)!**

Serves 10

Ingredients:
1 Cup grated carrot
1/2 Cup onions, fried
1/2 Cup flat leaf parsley, chopped
1 Cup grated parmesan
4 Cups strong bread flour
2 Sachets easy yeast
1 tsp Sea salt
1 tbsp Sugar
Warm water

Method:
1. Mix all ingredients with warm water in mixing bowl to firm consistency.
2. Knead well for about 10 minutes.
3. Allow to prove for 1 hour.
4. Knock back and leave for a further 1/2 hour.
5. Roll out into rolls or 2 loaves.
6. Bake in oven for 35 to 40 minutes on gas mark 7.

Desserts

Pumpkin Pie

We served this pumpkin pie recipe on our very first Supper Club night, with cream or custard and it was pure delight! We use pumpkins in sweet and savoury dishes in the Caribbean as it's a very versatile vegetable with a slightly sweet taste.

Serves 8

Ingredients:
1 Pumpkin
2 Whole eggs and 1 egg yolk, beaten
8 oz Light soft brown sugar
1 tbsp Plain flour
½ tsp Salt
1 ½ tsp Ground cinnamon
1 tsp Ground ginger
½ tsp Ground nutmeg
½ tsp Ground allspice
1 tsp Vanilla extract
12 fl oz Evaporated milk
Ready-made pastry, cut to 23 cm diameter

Method:
1. Cut pumpkin in half, remove seeds.
2. In baking tray lined with greaseproof paper, place pumpkin cut side down.
3. Bake in oven for 40 to 50 minutes on gas mark 6 or until flesh of pumpkin is tender when skewered.
4. Remove from oven and cool, enough to enable handling.
5. Scoop out flesh from peel, discarding the skin.
6. Mash flesh, a blender or potato ricer can be used.
7. Measure out 500g pureed pumpkin.
8. Reset oven to gas mark 8.
9. Line pie dish with pastry.
10. In mixing bowl, place all the ingredients. Stir well until all are blended together – a food processor can be used.
11. Pour mixture into pastry lined dish.
12. Bake in oven for 10 minutes at gas mark 8.
13. Reduce oven temperature to gas mark 5 and bake for a further 50 minutes or until when a skewer is inserted when removed clean.
14. Leave to cool before serving.
15. Serve with whipped cream or custard.

Tip:
This dish is best made the day before serving. It allows all the flavours to develop.

Nutmeg Ice Cream

Nutmeg is one of our favourite spices we use a lot of in Carriacou, Grenada. Adding it to ice cream only makes it more yummy in this sumptuous recipe!

Serves 8

Ingredients:
500ml Ready-made custard (really good quality one)
350 ml Double cream
1 Tin Condensed milk
1 tsp Vanilla extract
1 tbsp Freshly ground nutmeg
Pinch of salt

Method:
1. In mixing bowl, place all ingredients and blend using a hand held whisk.
2. Whisk until thickened.
3. Place mixture into lidded plastic container and freeze.
4. An ice cream maker can be used, follow manufacturer's instructions.

Desserts
Mango & Mint Sorbet

If you want a refreshing dessert, then this is the recipe for you. (It's also great for your breath too!)

Serves 6

Ingredients:
4 Ripe mangos peeled, stoned and chopped
3 tbsp Fresh mint chopped
300g Icing sugar
Juice of 3 limes
2 tbsp Rosewater

Method:
1. Place all ingredients into a food processer, blend to a pureed stage.
2. Remove from blender and churn in an ice cream maker according to manufacturer's instructions.
3. Transfer to a lidded container and store in freezer until ready to serve.

Tip:
Can be placed into a container after blending in food processor and freeze, then forking or whisking after 2 to 3 hours on 2 occasions.

Monica's Coconut Cake

This cake has always been very popular within my family for many years. It's lovely and moist and tastes great with a nice cup of tea or coffee.

Serves 8

Ingredients:
350g Self raising flour
2 tsp Baking powder
350g Butter
350g Caster sugar
6 Eggs Lightly beaten
100g Desiccated coconut
Finely grated zest and juice 3 limes
1 tsp Vanilla extract
½ tsp Ground cinnamon
½ tsp Ground nutmeg
¼ tsp Salt
100 ml Sugar syrup

Method:
1. Preheat oven at gas mark 6.
2. Grease 10" cake tin.
3. In mixing bowl, cream together butter and sugar.
4. Beat into the butter and sugar mixture the beaten eggs, zest and juice of limes and vanilla extract.
5. Blend all dry ingredients together.
6. Fold in dry ingredients into butter mixture until blended well.
7. Place mixture into 10" cake tin.
8. Bake in oven for 50 to 55 minutes or until when a skewer is inserted it comes out clean
9. Remove from oven, cover with sugar syrup, cool in tin on wire rack before removing.

Jamaican Rum & Raisin Ice Cream

We always put a good shot of rum into this ice cream! Why not grate some fresh nutmeg over the ice cream before serving, it tastes super!

Serves 10

Ingredients:
500ml Ready-made custard (a good quality one)
350ml Double cream
350ml Condensed milk
Pinch salt
2 tsp Vanilla extract
½ tsp Nutmeg
1 Cup Raisins
¼ Cup any Jamaican rum

Method:
1. In mixing bowl, place all ingredients, whip together until thickened, using a hand blender.
2. Place into a lidded container and freeze until ready to serve.

Tan Rosie's Ginger Cake

This is another firm favourite from our Supper Club events. The ginger syrup makes a big difference to the cake, giving it extra moisture and yumminess! It tastes great with ice cream or vanilla cream too!

Serves 8

Ingredients:

250g Butter
4 eggs, Lightly beaten
4 tbsp Grated root ginger
1 tsp Vanilla extract
200 ml Milk
4 tsp Baking powder
320g Plain flour
4 tsp Ground ginger
1 ½ tsp Ground cinnamon
½ tsp Salt
275g Soft dark brown sugar
2 Pieces stem ginger sliced thinly
100 ml Sugar syrup (syrup from stem ginger can be used)

Method:

1. Preheat oven to gas mark 6
2. Grease 9" cake tin
3. In mixing bowl, cream together butter and sugar.
4. Add beaten eggs, continue to mix well, add milk, vanilla extract and grated ginger and mix.
5. Mix all dry ingredients together and add to the butter mixture and fold in.
6. Pour batter into greased cake tin.
7. Place in oven and bake for 60 minutes or until when skewer is inserted it comes out clean when removed.
8. Remove from over, decorate with sliced stem ginger, drizzle over ginger syrup and allow to cool.

Guava & Apple Crumble

Adding a Caribbean fruit to a traditional English dessert can really transform your dish! Guava tastes perfect next to apples. Expect very clean bowls afterwards!

Serves 10

Ingredients:
2 Cups Guava, de seeded and chopped
2 Cups Apples chopped
½ tsp Ground cinnamon
¼ Cup Sugar
For Crumble topping
1 Cup Flour
1 Cup Oats
250g Butter
½ tsp Salt
½ Cup Sugar
½ tsp Ground cinnamon

Method:
1. Preheat oven to gas mark 7
2. Grease dish
3. In mixing bowl, add guava, apples, cinnamon and sugar, mix together.
4. Pour fruit mixture into dish and set aside.
5. To make crumble, place flour salt and butter into mixing bowl, rub in mixture to fine bread crumbs.
6. Add sugar, oats and cinnamon and mix well together.
7. Spread crumble mixture over fruit mixture.
8. Bake in oven for 50 minutes.
9. Remove from oven.
10. Serve with cream or custard

Desserts
Bolo Boracho
(Tipsy Rum Cake)

This is another fab Cuban recipe that we served up for very happy guests! The rum syrup is very important to add extra flavour and moistness to the cake.

Serves 8

Ingredients:
3 Cups Plain flour
3 tsp Baking powder
1 ½ Cups Softened butter
1 Cup Heavy cream
5 eggs Lightly beaten
1 ½ Cups Light brown sugar
Zest of 1 Lemon or lime
1 Cup Dark rum
2 tsp Vanilla extract
½ tsp Ground cinnamon
½ tsp Ground nutmeg
¼ tsp Salt

For rum syrup:
1 Cup Sugar
½ Cup Water
¾ Cup Dark rum
¼ Cup Butter

Method:
1. Preheat oven to gas mark 6
2. Grease 10" cake tin
3. In mixing bowl, cream together butter and sugar.
4. Add beaten eggs and mix well.
5. Add heavy cream, rum and zest of lemon and mix.
6. Mix all dry ingredients together and fold into batter mixture.
7. Pour batter into cake tin. Bake in oven at gas mark 6 for 60 minutes or until when skewer is inserted in cake and removed clean.
8. Remove from oven and leave in cake tin to cool.

To make rum syrup:
1. Place saucepan on hob on medium heat.
2. To saucepan add water and sugar.
3. Bring to the boil, reduce heat and simmer for 5 minutes until sugar is melted.
4. Remove from heat, add butter and whisk, add rum and continue to whisk until blended.
5. With a skewer make some holes in cake and pour over rum syrup.
6. Leave for at least 3 days until flavours develop.

Tip:
Some extra rum can be spooned over cake for a more tipsy cake.

Tropical Fruit Salad

You can't beat a great fruit salad that's simple and fresh to round off a great meal and this combination will not disappoint!

Serves 4

Ingredients:
1 Fresh mango peeled, stoned and sliced
½ Fresh pineapple skinned, cored and sliced
1 Papaya peeled, de seeded and sliced
½ Cup Pomegranate seeds
Few mint sprigs for garnish

Method:
1. Layer ingredients into individual serving bowls, garnish with mint leaves and serve.

Drinks

Rum Punch

Fond memories of sitting on Paradise beach in Carriacou Grenada come flooding back whilst drinking this rum punch! If you are in Carriacou, try using the local Jack Iron Rum instead of regular white rum, but be careful - it's very potent!

Ingredients:
3 Cups White rum
3 Cups Pineapple juice
3 Cups Orange juice
2 Cups Sugar syrup
¼ Cup Grenadine
¼ tsp Nutmeg
1 tsp Angostura bitters
Ice cubes

Method:
1. Place all ingredients into large jug and stir.
2. Serve with a sprinkling of nutmeg on top.

Monica's ~Drinks~ Ginger Drink

We normally serve my ginger drink as a complimentary drink for our Supper Club guests. After one glass, people generally want to drink the whole jug, so be warned - make more!

Ingredients:

8oz Fresh ginger peeled and chopped
2 Cups Sugar
3 litres Water
Juice and zest of 3 lemons
1 Stick cinnamon
1 tsp Angostura bitters
Ice cubes to serve

Method:

1. Place ginger with 1 litre of water in blender and puree.
2. Transfer to large saucepan; add rest of water, sugar, cinnamon and zest of lemon.
3. Bring to the boil over medium heat.
4. Reduce heat and simmer for 10 to 15 minutes.
5. Remove from heat, add lemon juice and Angostura bitters, stir.
6. Cover saucepan and let ginger drink cook.
7. When cold, strain using muslin cloth or fine sieve.
8. Serve with ice cubes.

Sorrel

Sorrel is a popular drink in the Caribbean made from the petals of the sorrel tree. You can buy them dried from Asian supermarkets and some larger supermarkets too. If you want an extra kick, add some rum!

Ingredients:
2 Cups Dried sorrel petals
4 Cups Sugar
3 litres Water
1 Stick cinnamon
3 Whole clove
2" Piece fresh ginger, sliced thinly

Method:
1. In large saucepan place all ingredients and bring to the boil stirring until sugar is dissolved.
2. Reduce heat and simmer for 15 minutes.
3. Turn off heat after 15 minutes and allow to cool
4. Strain using sieve or muslin cloth.
5. Pour into sterilised bottles and refrigerate.
6. Serve with ice cubes when ready.

Drinks

Lime Juice Rum Punch

This is a very refreshing Carriacouan drink to accompany any meal. You can omit the rum to make a virgin lime punch.

Ingredients:
2 ½ Limes
200gm Sugar Syrup
500ml Water
Nutmeg
Ice
Mint
100ml Grenadian Rum

Method:
1. In a tall jug add ice
2. Then add juice of 2 limes, sugar syrup, water and stir
3. Add slices of lime, sprig of mint, grated nutmeg and a couple of shots of Rum
4. Pour into tall glass and enjoy!

Supper Club Menus

Grenada

Grenada is a part of the Windward Islands in the Caribbean. Grenada is affectionately known as 'The Spice Island' due to the abundance of nutmeg and mace that is grown on its shores. It's one of the largest exporters of this precious spice which can be used in cooking or for medicinal purposes.

Grenadian food is a mixture of African, Indian and native Caribbean cuisine, to name a few. Due to the climate, alot of the meat and fish are 'corned' or salted to preserve them. Salted meat and fish are used in various Grenadian dishes.

Limes are one of the citrus fruits that are grown in Grenada and it's other parishes such as as Carriacou. They are used to clean meat and fish and they are added to juices and many other dishes.

Grenada's national dish is Oildown (page 41) which is a stew consiting of dumplings, salted meats, callaloo, breadfruit, chicken and other vegetables. It's then cooked in coconut milk with other spices such as nutmeg and allspice.

The menu overleaf is a mixture of some traditional dishes along with our own interpretations. We hope you'll enjoy trying them!

Tan Rosie

Caribbean Supper Club
Come & Dine In Our Living Room!

Grenadian Kitchen

Appetizer

**Corn Fritters & Sweet Potato Fritters
with a Spicy Lime Sauce
&
Complimentary Grenadian Rum Punch Cocktail**

Starter

**Salt Fish on a bed of Coo Coo (Polenta)
&
Traditional Home Baked Bread**

Main
**Traditional Rice & Peas (Pigeon Peas) with Curry Mutton
or
Channa Dhal (Chick Pea & Potato Curry) with plain rice**

Side dishes: Steamed Broccoli, Carrots & Fried Plantain
Dessert

**Pumpkin Pie with Fresh Cream
or
Nutmeg Ice Cream**

Shhhh... It's A Secret!

Trinidad

Trinidad is a part of the Leeward Islands in the Caribbean. It's smaller sister island is Tobago.

Trinidad cuisine contains a vast array of culinary influences from Africa, India, China, Portugal and native Caribbean. Trinidad has many popular dishes such as 'Doubles, ' Shark & Bake' and 'Macaronie Pie' (page 64).

The Indian influence on Trinidads' cusine is very strong. Trinidadians love their curries, rotis and dhals. There are a variety of different rotis from Trinidad that taste fantastic. Our favourite is 'Paratha Roti' or 'Buss Up Shut' (page 50). This particular roti consists of layers which is then torn up and pulled apart and served with a curry with plently of sauce.

We've included a few traditional Trinidadian recipes in our menu overleaf, but there are so many more fantastic recipes out there to try also - hopefully

Caribbean Supper Club
Trinidadian Kitchen

Appetizer

Phoulourie & Accras (Fritters)
served with
Spicy Banana Chutney & Tamarind Sauce

Complimentary Homemade Ginger Beer

Starter

Stuffed Plantains with Spinach

Main

Geera Pork with Buss-Up-Shut (Roti)
OR
Spicy Aubergine & Sweet Potato Bake

SIDE DISHES:

Macaroni Pie
Steamed Green Beans & Carrots

Dessert

Mango & Mint Sorbet
OR
Tan Rosie's Ginger Cake with Fresh Cream

Shhhh... It's A Secret!

Cuba

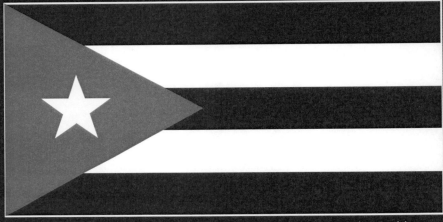

Cuba is a Spanish speaking island and it's one of the largest in the Caribbean.

Cuba's main culinary influence is Spanish and African. Ingredients such as rum, black beans and olives are used in a variety of dishes.

Cuban cusine is very simple. Cubans don't usually use alot of chillies in their food. As with other Caribbean islands, they use alot of root vegetables such as yucca and sweet potatoes.

Stews and soups are very common. These are normally eaten with rice or on their own.

Cuban sandwiches are a popular lunchtime meal utilising meats, poultry, cuban bread and cheeses.

The base of most sauces and stews is called 'Sofrito'. This is a sauce consisting of garlic, onions and tomatoes it can be added to almost any dish.

The most popular sauce is called 'Mojo' (page 22). This is a sauce made from oil, garlic, onion and other spices. It can be combined with other fruits such as mango to create some great tasting sauces.

Have a look at the menu overleaf for some great ideas for your Cuban menu!

Caribbean Supper Club

Cuban Kitchen

Appetizer

Mariquitas de Plátanos
(Plantain Crisps) with Salsa dip

Starter

Pure de Calabaza
(Creamy Pumpkin Soup)

Main

Pollo Borracho with Arroz Amarillo
(Drunken Chicken with Yellow Rice)

OR

Frijoles Negros & Bonito Bake
(Black Bean & Sweet Potato Bake)

Side Dishes: Steamed Brocolli & Carrots

Dessert

Monica's Cuban Rum Cake
with Cream or Custard

Shhhh... It's A Secret!

Jamaica

Jamaica is located in the northern part of the Caribbean and takes culinary influences from the native Caribbeans, Africa, Spanish and Chinese to name but a few.

Many of you will be familiar with some Jamaican dishes which include, Jerk Chicken (page 52) and Ackee & Salt Fish (page 32). Other popular dishes include Escoveitch fish which is made with lime juice, Fish Tea (soup) the list goes on!

Jerk is a very poplar marinade and style of cooking in Jamaica. Meat is marinaded with a wet sauce or dry seasoning rub. It is traditionally cooked on large open fires using particular varieties of wood which helps to give the meats a very unique flavour. More recently oil drums are converted into barbecues which are used by street stalls and during carnival to roast the various jerk pork and chicken dishes.

We've combined a selection of traditional Jamaican dishes with our own variations.

Have a go at the menu!

112.

Caribbean Supper Club

Jamaican Kitchen

Appetizer
Sweet Potato Crisps with Sweet Lime Sauce

Starter
Ackee & Salt Fish with Fried Dumplings

Main
Curry Goat with Rice & Peas
OR
Ital Stew with Rice (veg)

Side Dishes: Steamed Green Beans & Carrots

Dessert
Ginger Cake with Cream or Custard
OR
Jamaican Rum & Raisin Ice Cream

 Shhhh... It's A Secret!

Barbados

Barbados is a very popular English speaking island in the Caribbean.

Typical Caribbean dishes such as 'Cou Cou' (polenta) and 'Salt Fish' are cooked slightly differently with additional ingredients. Barbadian or 'Bajan' Cou Cou is made with okras which gives the dish a very different twist compared to the other Caribbean recipes.

Flying Fish and Cou Cou is a Bajan national dish which is eaten by the locals especially on national holidays. Their main source of protein is fish including, shark, tuna, flying fish, snapper and king fish. Bajan's enjoy a variety of different 'salted' fish along with many other Caribbean islands.

Bajan's love their desserts such peanut brittle, tamarind balls (tamarind is a fruit) and coconut bread.

Bajan's use a wide variety of fruit and vegetables in their cooking including: plantains, breadfruit, okras, christphene (a sugarless fruit), limes and cassava. They love their hot sauces of which they use in a variety of dishes!

Enjoy trying our Bajan menu ideas!

114.

Tan Rosie

Caribbean Supper Club
Come & Dine In Our Living Room!

Bajan Kitchen

Appetizer

**Cassava Crisps with
Pineapple & Mint Sauce**

Starter

**Cou Cou (polenta) with
Fried Red Snapper**

Main

Bajan Beef Stew with Coconut Rice

OR

Macaroni Pie with Spiced Tomato Sauce

Side Dishes: **Steamed Brocolli & Carrots**

Dessert

Guava & Apple Crumble
with Cream or Custard

OR

Fresh Tropical Fruit Salad

Shhhh... It's A Secret!

Aruba

Aruba is located in the southwestern part of the Caribbean and is a part of the Dutch Leeward Islands. Aruba is very close to Curacao and Bonaire.

Aruba takes it's culinary influences from the Dutch, Spain, Africa and native Caribbean people.

Arubans eat alot of stews, soups and fish such as Shrimps, Calamari, Shark, Swordfish and Conch.

Popular Aruban dishes include: Balchi di Pisca (salt cod balls page 29), Cala (bean fritters), Stoba (goat stew), Sopa di Pompuna (a pumpkin dish) and Keri Keri (a popular dish made from green peppers, fish, celery, onions and basil leaves).

We hope you enjoy trying our Aruban influence menu. You can easily swap out any ingredients to suit your taste when trying these recipes. Good luck and enjoy!

116.

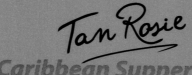

Tan Rosie

Caribbean Supper Club
Come & Dine In Our Living Room!

Aruban Kitchen

Appetizer

Yucca, Plantain & Sweet Potato Crisps
with Mango Mojo Sauce & Chilli Lime Sauce

Complimentary Virgin Sorrel Drink

Starter

Balchi di Pisca
(Salt Cod Balls) with Tamarind Sauce
& Homemade Bread and Side Salad

Main

Spicy Slow Roast Leg of Mutton

OR Veg. Option

Caribbean Style Nut Roast
with Onion Gravy

Side Dishes: Rice & Peas, Roasted Sweet Potato
Steamed Vegetables

Dessert

Bolo Boracho
(Tipsy Rum Cake) with Cream or Custard

OR

Caribbean Fruit Platter

Shhhh... It's A Secret!

Weights & Measurements

Gas Mark	Fahrenheit	Celsius	Description
1/4	225	110	Very cool/very slow
1/2	250	130	---
1	275	140	cool
2	300	150	---
3	325	170	---
4	350	180	---
5	375	190	---
6	400	200	moderate
7	425	220	hot
8	450	230	---
9	475	240	very hot

1 tablespoon (tbsp) =	3 teaspoons (tsp)
1/16 cup =	1 tablespoon
1/8 cup =	2 tablespoons
1/6 cup =	2 tablespoons + 2 teaspoons
1/4 cup =	4 tablespoons
1/3 cup =	5 tablespoons + 1 teaspoon
3/8 cup =	6 tablespoons
1/2 cup =	8 tablespoons
2/3 cup =	10 tablespoons + 2 teaspoons
3/4 cup =	12 tablespoons
1 cup =	150gm
8 fluid ounces (fl oz) =	1 cup
1 pint (pt) =	2 cups
1 quart (qt) =	2 pints
4 cups =	1 quart
1 gallon (gal) =	4 quarts
16 ounces (oz) =	1 pound (lb)
1 milliliter (ml) =	1 cubic centimeter (cc)
1 inch (in) =	2.54 centimeters (cm)

Capacity		Weight	
1/5 teaspoon	1 milliliter	1 oz	28 grams
1 teaspoon	5 ml	1 pound	454 grams
1 tablespoon	15 ml		
1 fluid oz	30 ml		
1/5 cup	47 ml		
1 cup 237 ml			
2 cups (1 pint)	473 ml		
4 cups (1 quart)	.95 liter		
4 quarts (1 gal.)	3.8 liters		